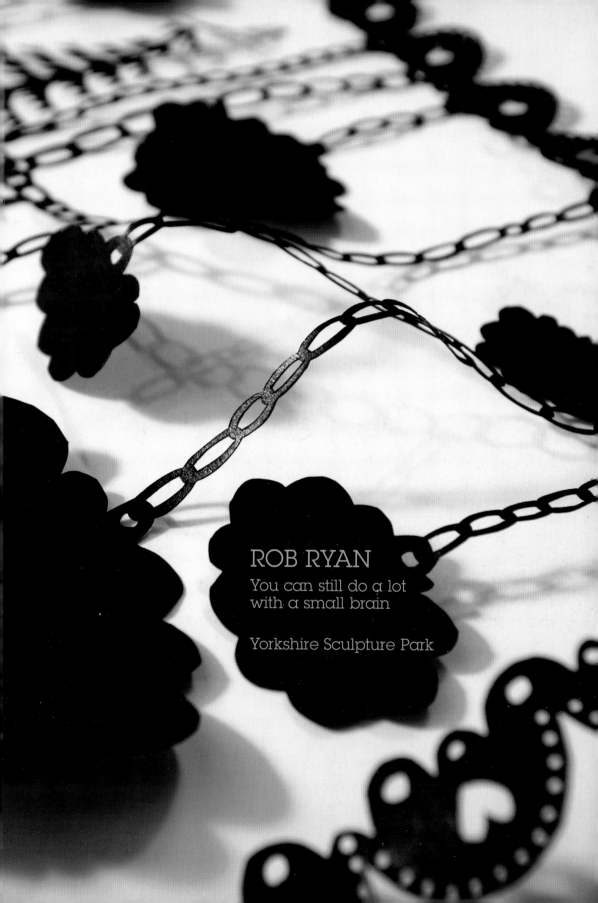

ROB RYAN

You can still do a lot
with a small brain

Yorkshire Sculpture Park

CONTENTS

PREFACE
AMANDA PEACH

Maybe it was my training as a surface pattern designer that initially drew me to the work of Rob Ryan. Maybe it was my fascination for the drawn line combined with pattern and colour. Whatever it was, I quickly developed a passion for Rob's work, became a regular visitor to his blog spot and started a growing collection of his whimsical gems, ranging from screenprints to clothing and a tea towel.

Rob trained as a fine artist at Trent Polytechnic in Nottingham and later went on to study an MA in Printmaking at the Royal College of Art. Since then he has developed an unmistakable style that is romantic and directly appealing. Rob is prolific in both his own artwork and his commercial work. His extraordinary ability to capture the zeitgeist is much sought after and he has worked for a string of notable clients such as Elle, Vogue and Velvet Magazines, Liberty's of London, and Fortnum and Mason; he has produced a range of fabrics and clothing with Sir Paul Smith, and stunning jewellery with Tatty Devine. He also shows his work internationally. I have long hoped to add Yorkshire Sculpture Park to this impressive list.

When the opportunity arose to stage a project throughout the Centre at YSP, possibly incorporating the imposing glass wall of the concourse, I immediately thought of Rob. Excited at the prospect of finally working together, I contacted him and, to my delight, he took up the challenge. Rob's schedule is such that he works around the clock, seemingly not finishing until he feels sure he can start the following day without feeling concerned about how much he has to do.

It was 24 April when Rob first visited YSP. He came across as a dedicated city dweller and I almost expected the 500 acre landscape of YSP to send him straight back down the motorway, yet he seemed to love YSP and its ethos, and made a commitment to work with us. Ideas started to form and the project grew rapidly in size, but Rob seems to relish producing work to a timescale and did not hold back on that account. I visited Rob at his Bethnal Green studio in May, experiencing on arrival a riot of colour, pattern and industry, almost as if I'd stepped into another world. In reality this isn't far from the truth – Rob has called his shop Ryantown and it has its own unique energy, look and dedicated band of inhabitants.

Copious meetings, emails and phone calls, research and ideas have culminated in the installation of a 22 metre wide by 4 metre high, intricately decorated vinyl window work, alongside framed works in the Upper Space, a commission to design a limited edition screenprint and a Christmas card. So, from November until February there will be a wonderful air of Ryantown about YSP.

I am most grateful to YSP Executive Director Peter Murray for the enthusiastic support and backing he has given to Rob's project. I would like to thank Clare Dwyer Hogg for her perceptive and beautifully written essay, also Sarah Coulson and Adrianne Neil for their help in organising the project and their engaging interview with Rob, and for Sarah's beautiful design of this book. Thanks also to Jonty Wilde for his stunning photographs, taken across Rob's two studios and shop, and at YSP.

Lastly, I offer my sincere thanks to Rob Ryan and his team, led by Hazel Nicholls. It has been an absolute pleasure to work with Rob and to witness his integrity and warmth while making something quite extraordinary for YSP.

ROB RYAN
CLARE DWYER HOGG

Fantastical swirling trees, flocks of birds making hieroglyphs in the air, bells that tell you they will ring when people are boring, and others that peal when love is in the air. Here is a place where stars hang from paper chains, buildings are inscribed with thoughts, leaves have faces and, hidden within nests, eggs hold important messages. This is a world where birds declare that an adventure is about to begin, and there are promises that something can come from nothing. A landscape that at a glance looks a bit like the one we see outside our window – but not quite. It's as if after years of looking out at a two-dimensional existence through the glass, we've finally chipped out the pane, climbed through the frame, and walked straight into the very heart of a three-dimensional world. And as our feet touch the dewy grass, it turns out that the glass we'd been staring through wasn't translucent, as it had seemed all along. Instead, it leeched out the imagination, took away emotion, so that all it left was a tree, staid in its rooted position, a bird travelling as the crow flies, an old church bell, silent, and stars that were just specks in the night sky. Not so, says Rob Ryan. The universe he cuts out from reams of paper is a fragile one, but it pulsates with life – and language. Words are essential in this world he's carved out: they give a visual voice to thoughts that would normally be locked internally, and allow creatures (usually birds) to speak, often with more wisdom than humans.

Rob Ryan started out as a painter. Yet as he developed as an artist, he found that words were creeping into his paintings. He did his best to ignore them, but they were persistent. "It reached a point where the paintings I did were just pages of writing," he told me, when I interviewed him recently for The Independent. But writing in paint wasn't the done thing. "People are funny about words in art," he said. "It's not that they think it's cheating..." He stopped. "Well, I think some people do think it's cheating you know." Rob tried not to cheat and began to run away from words as fast as he could. Still they dogged him. So because he couldn't stop himself writing in paint, he decided to try another medium. Paper cutting wasn't a lauded form, and there was something primitive and basic about it, so he went back to the drawing board and decided to make art that way. Cutting images into paper, his logic ran, would necessarily shut words out. "I thought if I did paper cuts that are folded and symmetrical then I couldn't write on them," he said. "Any words when you open them out would be back to front and they'd look ridiculous."

Yet art has an uncanny way of working around logic, and it turned out that paper cutting just wasn't enough of a bulwark. "I was inventing a way of not being able to write," he admitted. "And then the words came back. I found a way of doing it." Somewhat innocuously, he found himself ditching symmetry so that he didn't need to fold the pages any more – and then, slowly but surely, words started to appear in his art again. Rob Ryan had started to write again, except this time with a scalpel knife. And when he did that, he found something strange: people liked it. In a way they hadn't when he was painting. "I could do a painting that could be heart-wrenching, throwing my guts on the gallery wall, and it would just hang there," he told me. "And then I could do a paper cut, a little flowery thing, saying the same thing, with the same imagery, and people can swallow it."

Perhaps because the 'flowery thing', something of beauty, is just a mode of transport, bringing us through bowers and trees and the words of a bird towards wild flights of fancy, or the deepest of blackest thoughts. Because the emotions expressed

THIS BELL WILL RING WHEN FROM NOTHING SOMETHING COMES

THIS BELL WILL RING WHEN WE DREAM A DREAM OF GOOD

This Bell Will Ring, 2009

in Rob's paper cuts are not always sweet or light. "Please God don't let me have too much" is the plaintive cry etched out in one, from a father resting in branches, playing with his two children. The fragility of happiness is poised on a knife-edge between too little and too much. And so, the same blade that spells out declarations of love in spindly letters that swing between branches also cuts to the heart of human despair: "I cried and I screamed at the sky I don't want to feel like this for the rest of my life," reads one anguished plea in the book This Is For You. "But the clouds were indifferent to my tears," it continues, "and why should they care..."

The vulnerability in the world Rob is uncovering – the breaths held for dreams to come true, the whispered confessions of loneliness – is aptly reflected in the medium he now uses to express it. Just as one rough handling of his paper cut could tear through letters and obfuscate the message, so it seems within the scenes he's carved out that one unexpected breeze, or an errant swirl of smoke from one of the long fairytale chimneys, could change everything. The key to his work is in observing details, in recognising the importance of the minutiae of existence. "Paper cutting means that you strip things down," the artist says. "Because everything is cut from one sheet of paper, it forces a form of decorative pattern – everything has to link together." For paper cutting to work, then, every detail – from the tiniest teardrop to each rung of a ladder that stretches to the sky – must be interlinked. In the same way, for Rob Ryan's paper world to pulsate with life, the emotions connected to those images must be meticulously documented. They illuminate the feelings between words, as inherent to the pictures as are the spaces between the images.

What Rob Ryan cuts out, then, shows us the places between the spaces, the meaning of shadows where thought-dreams are revealed, and the liminal spaces where hopes and fears are articulated. What appears with the slice of a knife is a world where poetry hangs from the trees, where words are entwined with bricks and mortar, and letters express feelings, as ethereal as a smoke message traced out in the sky, yet as vital as breath itself.

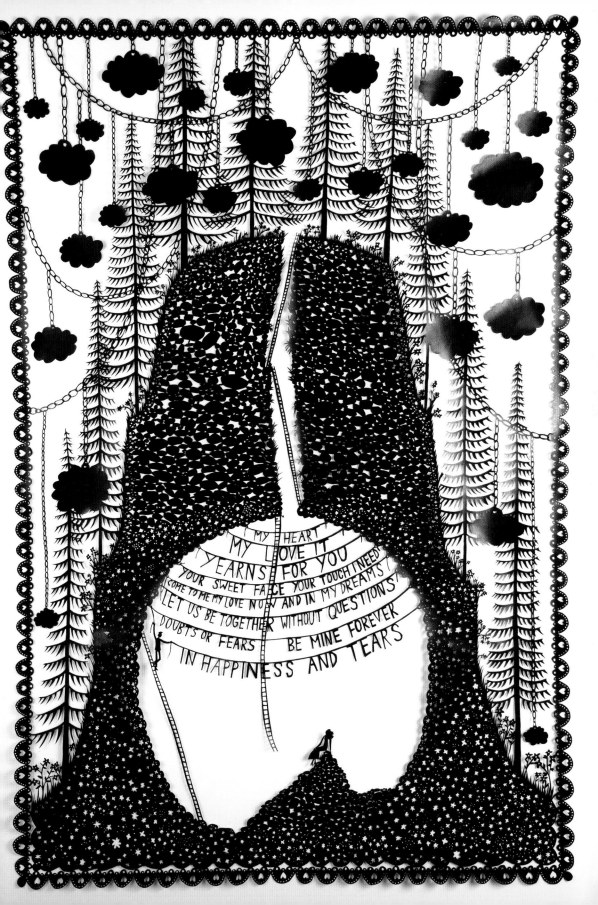

Centre, Yorkshire Sculpture Park
11 window decals
each panel 4.5 metres high x 1.9 metres wide

You can still do a lot with a small brain, 2009

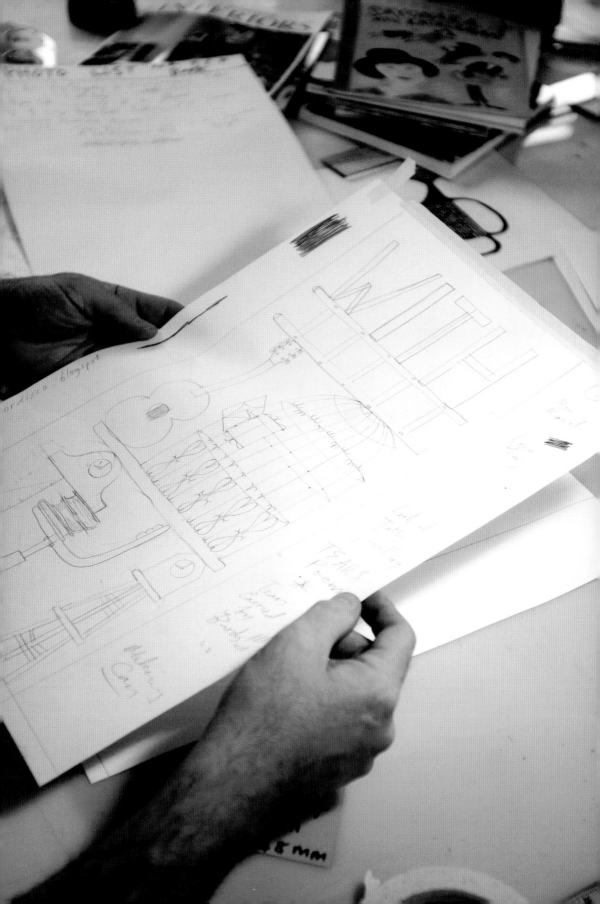

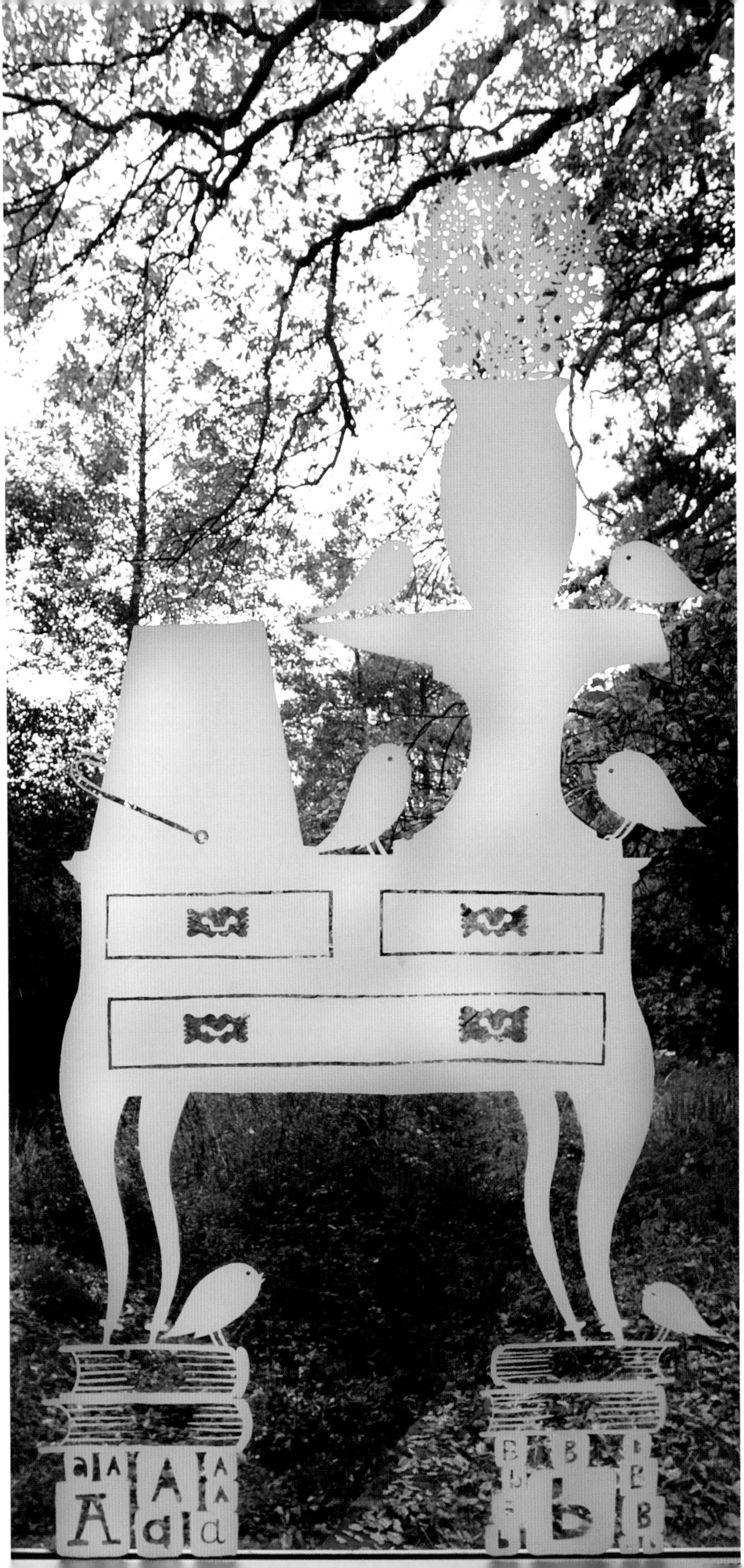

ROB RYAN: INTERVIEW
SARAH COULSON & ADRIANNE NEIL

SC: The installation you have made for the concourse windows at YSP is quite different to much of your work, which typically features very lyrical landscape settings. Here we see modern and traditional furniture and domestic objects – a rocking chair, an anglepoise light, a fringed standard lamp, an iron – can you say something about your choice of this particular subject matter?

RR: This piece is something quite new and different for me. It is my first window decal piece and the first piece of work that I have made covering such a large area. All of the objects that fill up this space, piled high and precariously, similarly fill our everyday lives. Though they are mundane when seen in isolation like this and out of their domestic context, they serve us faithfully and represent our days, our lives. The exciting thing about the large scale of this space is that these objects can be shown more or less actual size, the same size that we relate to them on an everyday basis.

SC: Some artists can feel overwhelmed when confronted with the vast landscape setting at YSP. Your work often references landscape in a very evocative, romantic and nostalgic way, but in reality you are based in the city and have an incredibly urban life. Why did you choose to avoid landscape when working on a commission for a rural setting? Did the reality of exhibiting in this very different kind of environment for you make you look to other ideas?

RR: Yes, I do live, and enjoy living, in the city. It would be as cruel and unusual to make a farmer live in the centre of London as it would be to make me live in the country. It is true though that I do romanticise the countryside in my work, it is a mental sanctuary of peace that I often seek refuge in and escape to in my work. With this being a window piece set in quite a narrow space there is not the chance for the viewer to step back and see the piece from any distance, it is almost impossible to see it properly as a whole.

The idea was to make something that revealed itself to you slowly as you walked past it; the individual spacing of the words in each panel means that the message is revealed slowly too. As such I hoped that the viewer would feel as if these objects were related more specially to them by being the same size. I think this is one of the reasons why I departed from my usual more pastoral themes – I wanted to use things that were human size, made for humans, made for hands and arms to hold and implement and elbows and knees to fit into and around; not exactly nature but things that exist because they were created to fit around the type of nature that is man and as such they are 'of nature' themselves.

AN: Do you think your work is sometimes seen as frivolous because you deal with romantic themes and imagery from nature?

RR: I'm sure that people do see my work as frivolous – and maybe it is. Frivolity, like sentimentality, seem to be descriptions that are considered derogatory – and I'm sure to some artists even insulting – but I don't see them like that at all. I don't think that the things I produce are lacking in seriousness, I think that a lot of the messages behind my work are as serious as any ideas I see being made in contemporary art.

SC: Hans Christian Andersen made little known but extraordinary paper cuts, many featuring figures involved in a narrative and incorporating text. He often used them as part of storytelling. How did you come to begin making paper cuts – were you aware of predecessors such as Andersen and the Nordic tradition for using paper cuts?

RR: Considering that I'm supposed to be a 'paper cutting artist' I really am very ignorant of all the other examples of the genre. For years I had a book of Swiss Tyrolean paper cuts made by folding the paper vertically, very symmetrical and ordered, cows with big cow bells around their necks, mountain scenes and chalet-like houses with picket fencing – totally perfect in its ordered simplicity. A whole world cut from a single piece of paper.

The only artist I was aware of at the time when I started working in paper was Kara Walker, of whom I'm a huge fan, but my work is fairly far removed from hers in both style and content. When I did begin to work in this way I think my little book of Swiss papercuts was my one and only reference and my first dozen or so pieces were all made from cutting folded over paper. However, this was really a foil to stop myself from using words in my work; up to this point my prints and paintings were becoming saturated with more and more words and stories to the extent that they were becoming totally covered in lettering with hardly any imagery. I felt that I had either to give up using words or just give up painting and write a book! By using mirrored symmetry it was impossible to have words because on one side of the work half of the words would come out back to front. However, the words did slowly come back of course…

SC: Your pieces featuring figures in a dialogue with both the landscape and themselves feel to me like a modern take on works such as those of Caspar David Friedrich, where the landscape is a foil for introspection – a timeless notion. Do you think that is true and do see yourself as keying into these kinds of ideas and traditions? In many ways it seems there are stronger links in approach between you and these artists than the paper cutting tradition.

RR: I am so happy that you have said this. People constantly ask me if I look at 'so and so' paper cutting artist – to tell the truth I have no particular interest in papercutting, but I love German Romanticism; Adolph Von Menzel's The Balcony Room is by far and away my favourite ever painting. I love Caspar David Friedrich (Moonrise Over the Sea and Wanderer Above the Mists), Karl

Frederick Schinkel (Medieval Town by Water, Morning, and The Banks of the Spree Near Stralau) and Johan Christian Dahl. Here the picture is so much about the silhouette, much more so than in paper cutting art which is principally concerned with decoration. Like so many Romantic paintings, my work is sentimental and wistful, the world is so big and wonderful and man is only this tiny figure standing in the forefront gazing in awe.

SC: Silhouettes pare back an image to the absolute minimum, yet in doing so have a real intensity. How much is the medium central to your explorations of emotion? Do you think that the form you use adds to the way the works communicate?

RR: Silhouettes, mainly because the shapes of figures are viewed in profile and are thus seen in isolation without anything shadowing their outline, perfectly freeze and highlight a gesture, a moment. There came a point when I didn't want to experiment with paint any more, moving it around the canvas endlessly, I just wanted to work with one shape. The things that I try to say are rarely complex, and on the contrary are usually very simple, indeed straightforward enough to make from a single piece of paper. Although time does seem sometimes to drag, all our lives are really quite momentary. In the grand scheme of things we are really only shadows ourselves.

SC: When I first saw your work I presumed that you used coloured papers for your papercuts. Now I realise that, in fact, you start with white paper which is then coloured. Can you explain the process through to the finished work?

RR: I have one paper I prefer to cut from. It's quite thin and very smooth and comes in quite a large size; it is used for printing large church Bibles. The papercuts are sprayed with colour after they are cut, which can be quite tricky sometimes because delicate parts blow up with the force of the spray and stick to each other.

The process is very simple – I draw the design onto the paper with a very sharp pencil and then I or an assistant will cut it out. After they are coloured we stick them down to a backing sheet of paper with tiny dabs of PVA, just enough to hang them up, they don't need much because they're very light.

AN: You've said that you come from a fine art background, does that mean you would describe yourself as a fine artist?

RR: There is something about the terms 'fine art' and 'fine artist' that has always made me feel slightly uncomfortable. I can imagine being asked at a party what I do for a living: "well actually, I'm a fine artist". The answer in my head always comes with a "well actually" attached. It automatically comes out sounding pretentious. But if the real definition of a true fine artist is someone who exclusively works on his or her own ideas, does not work on commercial projects, does not collaborate and is free from compromise, true only to themselves and their own artistic integrity then surely that must be a wonderful thing – but it's not me.

I studied fine art at college for six years and I remember when I started seeing for the first time very serious young men, some with beards, many with well worn editions of Penguin Classics sticking out of the back pockets of their navy blue workmen's trousers, very busy setting out their store as fine artists. They were all the best part of 19 years old, but they were very serious about being serious. The problem with me is I don't feel very serious-minded at all, I consider myself silly. I'm not dignified, I feel more ridiculous than anything. I consider myself shallow rather than deep. Who would want to be at the snobby party at Omega House? I'd want to be at the Delta House party having fun – I'd want to be in Animal House!

SC: You were at the Royal College of Art – what did you specialise in and did anyone there have a particular influence on you as an artist?

RR: Not especially. Sometimes you have experiences that are more beneficial to you because they help you realise more clearly what you <u>don't</u> want to do. I knew that I didn't want to end up a lecturer in an art college, an ambition that a lot of my contemporaries had their sights set on. The real reason for going to the RCA is, of course, because of the wonderful technicians and benefiting from their incredible expertise.

AN: Because of the nature of some of the projects you have undertaken, such as magazine covers, book sleeves etc, do people often describe you as a graphic designer? Are you comfortable with this description?

RR: I have never understood why some people would consider me a graphic designer, but I do get called that all the time. I don't know the first thing about graphic design and I'm not interested in doing so at all.

I guess because I use words in my work it in some way makes me a part of the graphic design / fine art debate. These days the boundaries between the two are so blurred as to make that kind of debate meaningless. I think it is an old fashioned way of thinking. Picasso said "I never do a painting as a work of art".

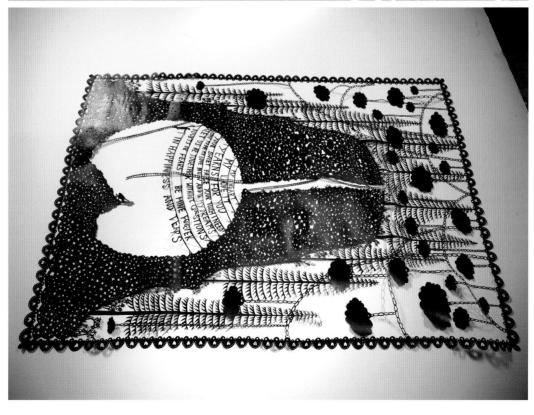

The real thing here is that people want to be able to call you something! Give you a label and file you neatly away somewhere. I can't do anything about what people want to call me – that's up to them. I don't feel particularly uncomfortable about it, but it might mislead some people. I think that to be any kind of an artist you must feel as if you have something to say, an urge to create, a passion, a desire. To make plates and bowls and t-shirts and wallpaper with things to say on them rather than on canvas isn't really going against the grain.

SC: You are currently working on illustrations for Carol Ann Duffy's forthcoming children's book 'The Gift'. How does this process work – do you receive a text and then have the freedom to develop your own ideas around it?

RR: This is the first book I've produced in collaboration with another writer. I receive the text which is finished and final. I break it down into how many pages they want the book to be. Then I begin to position the type on the page with some very rough sketches of how the pictures and words will work together. This is then emailed to the publisher and their designer who give feedback, changes and suggestions, and it gets hammered out back and forth like that for a while until we are all happy with it. The author only sees it when it's finished. When we're all happy with the layouts I start doing detailed pencil roughs of each page or double page spread, and then this is emailed to the publisher. If any changes are requested we discuss this and they are made (or not).

Then I have the go ahead to cut: because the paper cuts can't be edited or changed we have to be absolutely sure that the image is what everyone wants. It's challenging, but it is a collaboration and that's the nature of it. The next book will be only my words and my pictures.

AN: You've done some high profile commercial projects but you seem to have a lot of control and creative freedom. Is work you submit ever rejected and, in that situation, would you re-submit?

RR: This is an iceberg that people rarely even see the tip of! In commercial projects the best clients are the ones who actually like and 'get' what you do – they realise that by giving you freedom to get on with it you will produce the best work for them. Paul Smith is a very good example.

At the other end of the spectrum there are clients that are aware of what you do and see the look and the style of it as something that is current or fashionable and they want a part of it – they don't really see what the work is saying, they just want you to interpret their own ideas in your style. With practice you get to work out who is who and back away from the latter. I don't like re-submitting work because it leads to more re-submitting and it can go on forever; in these cases it is best to stand firm or just walk away early on. Perversely, I do actually enjoy getting pissed off with jobs and clients, it might sound weird but it's like life, it's a challenge and it can be fun working through it. In my studio every day I scream and shout if things aren't working out – but it's mixed up with a lot of laughter too. It's all in a day's work – you just try not to take these small rejections personally and rise above it, like life.

AN: You clearly have many different strands to your practice. Are you able to explain how those strands relate to and inform one another?

RR: There is quite a wide variety to the things that I do, but to tell the truth I don't see all these strands as ever being separate identities on their own, nor do I see them as being neatly woven together harmoniously. I see them much more like a big tangle of Christmas tree lights that are far too much effort to separate so you just plug them in and enjoy the whole big bundle! I used to consider some of it as more commercial and some of it more personal work, but these days I just see

Rob Ryan collaboration with Paul Smith, 2006

it all as my work and don't worry about it. For example, something I produced for an editorial illustration for an Italian newspaper's horoscope page – a part of that may spring up half a year later in a major paper cut piece, and vice versa.

I think that if you begin to separate the work that you produce for people into different levels of importance then you start delivering different levels of quality in your work and you end up selling people short. It's not easy but you have to try and do the best job for everybody, including yourself.

SC: When we last met you mentioned the idea that all artists exist as a brand – how do you feel about this and do you feel it is a method of survival in a field where it can be difficult to earn a living.

RR: Well. It's a Warholian statement that when first made probably sounded quite radical, but in time has actually come to pass. Art is no longer seen as a 'higher calling' but much more as a commodity. You make something, you don't do it anonymously, you put your name to it. Obviously the more that people are familiar with you and what you do then the more they are ready to accept you second and third time around, that's the nature of branding. But it's not necessarily about money, it can be as simple as an idea resonating with people, a thought or a feeling that stays with you. Sometimes I remember something I read or heard or saw twenty years ago, as often as two or three times a week – something that made sense to me, and for some reason I've held on to it for a large part of my life.

AN: Do you think that your practice is often put into the bracket of craft/design because it has a lot to do with the process of making and there is a learned skill that is crucial to it?

RR: I think that a lot of what artists do is very highly skilled, the result of many years' practice and is often undervalued. I think it's more to do with people's attitude to objects, if they have a usefulness to them like, for instance, a cup and saucer or something you can wear like a scarf, then you may be considered a 'craftsperson' rather than an 'artist'. If you make a cup with a hole drilled in the bottom then it is of course 'art' and should be in a gallery. I think I'm heading into conceptual territory here...

AN: You've had a shop near to your studio for a couple of years now – has this altered the way you work and the artwork you produce?

RR: My shop was never intended to be the beginning of anything bigger than what it already is, it was always meant to be a fun thing. Because it is only a five minute walk from my studio the idea was that it was a place where I could try things out for the sake and joy of making them and having a place in which to show them to people. Things that were not commissioned, things where I don't have to worry about which outlet would be interested in selling them – a place where I could be free to experiment. I thought that because I have my own screenprinting studio I could produce very new, fresh things all the time for the shop. The beauty of taking control of the means of production is that, for example, you could be sitting up in bed on a Thursday night and have a great idea for a new tile design, draw it up on Friday morning, have the artwork put on screen by lunchtime, print in the afternoon, fire in the kiln overnight and take them out HOT on Saturday morning to have in the shop for when it opens at lunchtime. This process for most designers/producers would take weeks if not months. In this way I envisaged the shop as having ever changing stock, not unlike 'fresh produce' in a grocer's shop. The ability to do such a quick turnaround always keeps me thinking and working to feed my mini 'ideas laboratory'! If you ever read David Hockney's 'Paper Pools' book you will see what I mean – he is totally inspired by the ability to work and create at speed.

AN: Do you think that this commercial aspect of your output will always prevent you from being considered by many as a fine artist? Is this distinction even an issue to you?

RR: Everybody on this planet, no matter how strenuously they deny it, is to some degree concerned with what people think about them – and I am one of the worst! But this is my personal mountain that I have to overcome. The most self-conscious person is sometimes the one who is most incredibly and outlandishly dressed – perhaps just to get over it, they have to go out and prove it to themselves. I would like people to look at and get something from my work. Whether or not some people don't deem it 'fine art' doesn't seem to me to have anything to do with that process.

AN: Is the shop less of a money making venture and more of an opportunity to disseminate your work to a wider public?

RR: The shop is not a great success if seen as an attempt at Rob Ryan world domination. It's small, it's situated in an out of the way street in East London, it's only open one and a half days a week and sells quite limited quantities of stock. These days I would say that the internet would be a much more ideal way to access a vast audience directly. The shop pays for itself and keeps in profit (so far). What I suppose is of interest is that it is a place where I can deal directly with the public without any kind of middle person involved. Because the work can and does relate to people on quite an emotional level the shop has a special level of intimacy, principally as it is all my work.

A customer recently said it's a bit like walking into someone else's brain. Where the shop does succeed is in how it bridges the gap between gallery and shop. No matter how grand and rarefied its premises or staff may be, to me even the most exclusive and expensive gallery is at the end of the day merely another shop. People can be intimidated in the gallery environment, it is quite a different shopping experience that most people are not used to. I am aware that a lot of people who buy screenprints from my shop for around £200 to £500 are making their first 'proper' art purchase. I think that people feel more relaxed and at ease to choose what they wish to buy because it seems like a shop rather than a gallery – the pressure is off. In reality it is both and neither.

SC: Your work is often filled with quite raw emotion, but is ultimately celebratory in its approach to life and love. How much of you is there in the work and how much do you see yourself as a writer charting wider issues in people's lives?

RR: I would be the first to put my hand up and say 'Yes I am a mess! I'm a neurotic, paranoid and self obsessed human', why else would any of these words and pictures I make exist? They are there solely to turn bad thoughts into good things, fears into hope. I don't feel as if I deliberately try and chart issues in other people's lives except that possibly we all secretly share the same fears and dreams, but we all keep them locked up inside ourselves. Knowing that somebody else understands you, thinks like you, is the greatest thing we can ever feel, this feeling is called love.

SC: Your portrayal of children is invariably touching and life-affirming – your line 'Why are you so naughty? Because I'm so happy' makes me smile when I think of my own son.

RR: That line is pointed at a child but I feel I would supply the same answer myself. I find it really hard to work out the whole adult-child thing – a lot of kids are like middle aged people and of course totally vice versa! When exactly do you change, finally become an adult? Personally, I don't feel it has happened to me yet. In my work I'm too busy looking forward towards the future and getting excited about what I'm going to be working on next. But then I'm not interested in what I am but what I will be.

RYANTOWN

126 COLUMBIA ROAD
LONDON E2

THE KEY TO MY HEART
NEVER DOUBTS AND NEVER WAVERS

THE KEY TO MY HEART
DOES NOT JUDGE OR HATE

THE KEY TO MY HEART
HAS HOPE THAT IS INDESTR-UCTIBLE

THE KEY TO MY HEART
KNOWS IT WILL ONE DAY BE FOUND

THE KEY TO MY HEART
LOCKS YOU IN FOREVER

Above: The Key To My Heart series, 2005. Opposite: We Had Everything, 2009

Above: Boat Couple, 2007. Opposite: Can We Shall We, 2009

Above: Where Are You, 2005.
Page 51/82: Our Adventure is About to Begin, 2004. For Amelia's Magazine.

EVERYTHING THAT IS... SU...

IS ALREADY H...

Everything That Is, 2009

Above: London Fashion Week, 2009. Opposite: I Can't Forget, 2008.

Opposite: We Don't Fly North (pink), 2008. Above: You Were In My Head, 2009.

TO MY DARLING
ALL OF THESE WORDS
ARE WORTH LESS THAN THE BREATH USED SAYING THEM
IF WE CANNOT BE TOGETHER
WHEN I WAKE UP IN THE MORNING I THINK OF YOU
WHEN I GO TO BED AT NIGHT PLEASE THINK OF ME
SOMEWHERE UNDER THE SAME MOON

32/40

This page: To My Darling, 2008. Opposite: My Home, 2009.

MY HOME
WILL HAVE
NO WINDOWS
DOORS OR FLOORS
NOR BRICKS
OR MORTAR.

MY
ONLY HOME
IS IN
YOUR ARMS
AND NOWHERE
ELSE.

EI

THE

HA   ALTH

SO   MES

WHE   EE

THE MANGLE

SCREENPRINTING STUDIO
KILN
SPRAYING PAPERCUTS

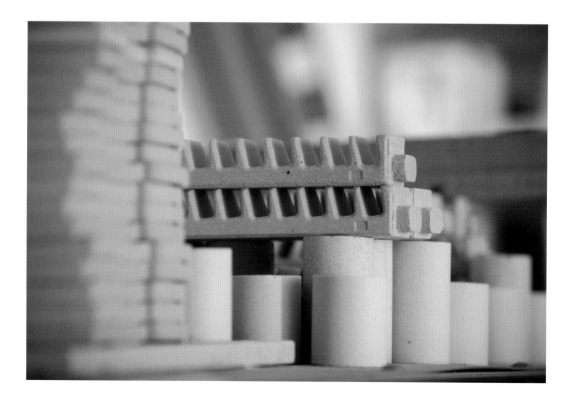

the wonderful story of
how ryan were born
&ryantown

The record
that solves
the problem of
answering your
child's questions

33⅓ rpm

Written and recorded by ROB RYAN

PAPER CUTTING
DECALS
ROB'S DESK

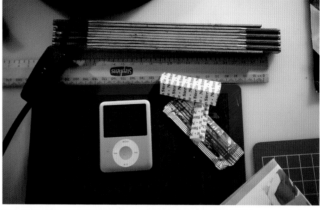

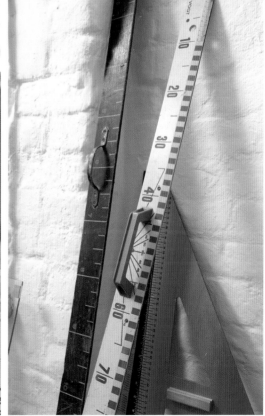

WHY DO THINGS HANG
DOWN FROM TREES IN MY
WORK ? Because it is a
TOPSY TURVY
way of seeing things.
Not the way they
really are.
THINGS THAT DONT
but COULD.
Things the ARN'T
but SHOULD.

Looking through a lot of old work I was desperate for an idea for a new paper ut, i know – it's pathetic! I was looking through a load of books & ~~treats~~ I found a few pages I painted plates that I had made and I saw what about ¾'s of these pictures had in common. They were all of people holding eachother, 2 boys with their arms around each other, A boy an girl holding hands, a chef balancing a small girl on his lap 2 men holding ~~each other~~ & throwing children up into the air. A man with one leg holding a woman 2 women holding a woman up in the air, A man lifting a girl up in the air at a train station 2 women holding cats on their laps. What is that trying to say ..... except HOLD ME, HOLD ME, HOLD ME, HOLD ME *Hold Me*

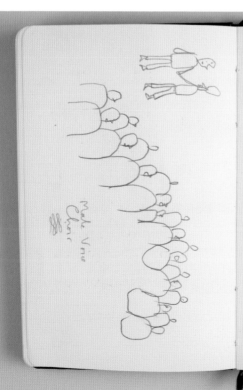

Made Vine
Choir

AND SO
IT ALL GOES

ON AND ON
AND ON AND
FOREVER AND
NOW I MUST
SAY GOODBYE
BECAUSE I'M PART
OF THE BOOK.

Published to coincide with

ROB RYAN
You can still do a lot
with a small brain

Yorkshire Sculpture Park
12 November 2009 – 21 February 2010

ISBN   978-1-871480-80-1

© the authors, photographer and Yorkshire Sculpture Park, 2009

Photography >   Jonty Wilde
Book design & production >   Sarah Coulson
Editing >   Sarah Coulson, Clare Lilley, Adrianne Neil
Proofing >   Angie de Courcy Bower, Adrianne Neil, Helen Pheby

Rob Ryan would like to thank his team: Hazel Nicholls, Sarah Withers, Suzie Winsor,
Cynthia Grandfield, Jackie Ford, Ellie Mulligan, Liberty Wright, Sarah McPhee,
Caroline Dulko, Eleanor Feddon, Aimee Snell, and Grace Ellington.

Yorkshire Sculpture Park
West Bretton > Wakefield > West Yorkshire > WF4 4LG
www.ysp.co.uk

01924 832631

As an independent art gallery, accredited museum and registered charity
(number 1067908), YSP's core work is made possible by investment from Arts
Council England, Wakefield Council, The Henry Moore Foundation and West
Yorkshire Grants.